V. Matt Harris

Money Grows On Trees: A quick, easy, simple guide to start growing your money today

Volume 1

Finding Opportunities for Financial Independence

© 2015 MGOT ENTERPRIZE. All rights reserved.

No copies in whole or part may be reproduced in any form without prior written consent of MGOT ENTERPRIZE.

sainttharris@gmail.com

Money Grows On Trees: A quick, easy, simple guide to start growing your money today

Revised Volume2 © 2016

Finding Opportunities for Financial Independence

© 2010 MGOT ENTERPRIZE. All rights reserved.

No copies in whole or part may be reproduced in any form without prior written consent of MGOT ENTERPRIZE.

contact us via email: sainttharris@gmail.com

Finding Opportunities for Financial Independence and associated logos are registered trademarks of MGOT.

MONEY GROWS ON TREES

A quick, easy, simple guide to start growing your money today

V. Matt Harris

CONTENTS

- ➢ PAID MONEY vs. MADE MONEY
- ➢ THE PERILS OF CHASING MONEY
- ➢ DEBT CREATORS
- ➢ EXPENSE & LIABILITY TREES
- ➢ WEALTH CREATORS
- ➢ ASSET & INCOME TREES
- ➢ EXPENSES vs. ASSETS
- ➢ ASSETS
- ➢ THE FARMER'S MENATLITY
- ➢ WATCHING YOUR MONEY GROW

PAID MONEY VS. MADE MONEY

Let me be very straight with you; "Paid money" belongs to someone else. You may be the owner of such money, it may have your name on it, and it may even be in your wallet or bank account, but the truth is that this money belonged to someone else and this person gave it to you. The person can choose to renegotiate with you and either give you more or give you... well, you guessed it; give you less.

You learn a trade or find work in order to get paid for your time and service. The person pays you because you are under his employ. He literally owns you based on that money that you are going to be paid. Napoleon Hill ,when citing the importance of thought, quoted "*a man is worth 2 dollars from the neck down*". I believe that using what you have *from the neck up* makes you worth much more.

"Made money" on the other hand does not belong to anyone. The same principles which apply when 'working' to earn money are not used. "Made money" has to be created with your head; meaning it is thought of, and so it comes "from the neck up". The service you provide, how you think, the actions you take will all be determining factors in what exactly you get back.

"Paid money" always has a cap. It can be lost or taken away. Remember, it is someone else's creation that's paying you. You are dispensable because you are not at the top of that food chain. The person at the top is giving you what he thinks you deserve.

"Made money" however can become limitless and residual. It will not stop coming even if you lose your job or experience some similar fate. You created it, so it is yours forever! It means investing services *from the neck up* and generating ideas which you must then put to good use and create some cash flow.

THE PERILS OF CHASING MONEY

Here are some quick stats for you:

- Do you know that about 98% to 99% of Americans chase moneyeveryday?This means that they have to wake up and go to work. They have to go and face their bosses.
- Only about 1-2% of Americans have figured out how to get money to chase them.

When you chase money through a job, you help in making your employer(s') dream(s) come true. More often than not, when you chase money, the more you get the more you tend to spend. Bigger houses, new cars, and expensive clothes (unless paid for in cash) really do nothing besides add to our debt and "job" dependence. Also just because you pay on the nail whenever you have an expense does not automatically make it the best decision; there are more factors involved to examine. "Jobs" are not designed to make your own personal dreams come true, and by no means will they make you a billionaire. I can't say with 100% assuredness that chasing anything will get you to it faster. I really try to see and feel myself in poession of whatever it is I'm desiring before anything. That way for me it doesn't feel so much like work.

Being overly committed to the "chase" will inevitably distract you from accomplishing your personal goals of financial independence, if indeed that is a goal. I am not saying to quit your job today! By all means be the standout employee. I just had to stop giving so much of my brain power to someone else. I knew I wanted more and had more to offer. Create some ideas or products for yourself! Theres something you love that someone else will too Made money is real, and can become residual once you start creating it. In the long run made money should provide more security than "paid money" and will definitely feel better.

DEBT CREATORS

As you strive to make some money for yourself, surely there will be some factors creating debts. Do not panic. This is in fact to be expected. If everyone only earned money without in the same vein accruing some debts, then there would be no poor man. Everyone would be pretty loaded with cash.

Have you ever taken time to just look at your account statement for a year? Just have your bank email it to you and you'll see what I mean. Do not look at the withdrawals or debits to the account. Only look at the credit section, and you may be shocked to find that in a year, almost a million dollars could have at some point 1 time or the other, been in your account.

However, because of the economic balance of life, debt creators must exist as well as you have credit creators. Let's have a look at some of the more notorious debt creators.

Expenses: The most widespread of all the debt creators. You always have to buy stuff. Whether it's food, work shoes, clothes for the kids or girlfriend or boyfriend or wife or husband, family; you are bound by nature to expend some money. Look at it like a loss for the sake of something gained; a cost.

TAXES: It is escapable, but you'll end up in jail. Tax evasion is now a serious offence, so if you treasure your freedom, its best you pay up your taxes and that is another debt creator for you.

Others may include; transportation, charitable causes, insurance and so on. I am sure if we put our heads to it we could name about 50 more debt creators. Expenses tend to compromise the every-day creation of money in an individual's life. With the exception of entertainment, they could be considered "the cost of living".

So we have to be attentive. Make wealth-conscious decisions. Feel good about starting a new train of thought. Making money can be so easy! For instance, spending 100 dollars for shoes whereas you could have spent 50 dollars for shoes. If you get the pair for 50 dollars, that is extra 50 dollars that you have created on the spot! The quickest way to get more "money" in your pocket is to immediately cut out unnecessary overages in your everyday spending. JUST GET THE 50 DOLLAR SNEAKERS!!! To me that's budgeting & an extra 50 dollars.

Million-dollar dreams have come to life with far less than a $50 investment. Once you get the money, put it up in the bank under a pillow somewhere. Give it a chance to grow, all the while thinking, imagining, focusing on something you can do with it to make more!

Once you begin to concentrate on creating more money it will become second nature and you'll see your expenses drop. Without a doubt if you do that, an opportunity will present itself. A major key to life is possessing a determined focus. A fierce tenacity that will push you to super-seed anything that life may throw at you.

Then there are liabilities and obligations, responsibilities or debts which also need to be curbed. It is easy not to count them among the debt-creators but they are in fact debt accumulators.

Mortgages, Consumer Loans, Credit Cards, I O Us, they are all the same thing. Debt. Are you obligated to any of these? They are the "major players" in the ruin-your-credit gang. After all the bills and expenses have been paid, your wallet can look like it was assaulted. Big houses with big payments that you struggle to keep up with, and make on time. They are of no real use to you. They are just pretentiously ostentatious and of no good. I do suggest a smaller house that allows you to save or at least sleep peacefully every night.

Do not cut up your credit cards, you do not need to. Simply get a grip on yourself. Control yourself.! If you have enough "chutzpah" to cut your card up, then you have what it takes to use it wisely; just do it. It may be difficult the first few times you opt out of using your credit card. After the first few days, as with anything else, it gets easier.

Remember, planting seeds of wealth should be your daily focus. Consciously choosing to not plant seeds of debt and plant seeds of wealth instead is setting you up for a great harvest of riches. Try it until you get it right just like a math problem or pronouncing a foreign word.

EXPENSE & LIABILITY TREES

So many of us have expense and liability trees in full bloom. If you spend time planting seeds of debt they may grow, and unlike seeds of success, they have a higher chance of growing successfully. You may have to eat that fruit with a grim face. It's called facing the music.

Of course the more debt seeds that you plant the longer it could take to get rid of them. Financial independence is always possible if that's what you want, and I mean really want. Expenses are like parasites that suck up all your money.

They can be found in car payments, high interest loans, credit cards and the like. Some debtsare unavoidable. For the small percentage of people making money however, it isavoidable. This is what we are all striving to become. That small percentage of people that make their own money. The percentage that harvests their money. The percentage that does not pluck from the expense and liability trees even though the expend money on a larger scale than those who are paid money. It all depends on what garden you plant in. The garden that creates debt or the garden that creates wealth.

Something i like to do before I make a purchase is what I call "walk away for a day". Most times the initial urge will subside to a different possibly more fulfilling purpose. In other words I generally realize it

Money Grows on Trees...

wasnt as important as I thought it was.

Peradventure, if after my "walk away a day", I still feel as strongly about the purchase then I may get it and not feel guilty.

WEALTH CREATORS

These are markers of wealth. A stable income, a steady uptick in the accumulation of assets without any of the aforementioned debt markers, stocks, bonds, notes, real estate, intangibles, intellectual property.

A job earns you a right to a paycheck, and a paycheck means that you are you are a recipient of "paid money" If you want to become a wealth creator, then you need to start thinking outside the box. Know that there is a life beyond jobs and the paycheck. A stable income combined with royalties, perhaps intellectual properties or financial investments, rental income and so on put you on the right path to success and creating wealth. If you are in possession of any of the aforementioned wealth creators, you already know the benefit of "made money".

As stated earlier, "made money" can become residual and does not stop at the loss of a job. Everyone has the opportunity to acquire wealth. Once you decide to, make an effort until it happens. Plant seeds of wealth. Take time to think of different ways to create "made money". The floodgates of your mind will eventually open. That creative juice will flow right out of your thinking faculty in ways which you did not anticipate. Once your mind 'unlocks'. You will see, and feel more money flowing into your pocket.

The wealth creator that every normal human being has been imbued with is their mind. We just need to get it off the default survival mode. There is not a single thing in the world that anyone can achieve without using someone else's idea. Think about it, from buttoning a shirt, reading this book or driving a car, someone had to think of it. What if you were to became more inventive and find the method to elevate your awareness. I mean really learn to use your number 1 wealth creator your mind where all your seeds are.

ASSET & INCOME TREES

I reeled off some statistics earlier in the book. Approximately 6-10% of the population controls nearly 96% of the wealth? That's about 4% for the rest of America to divide. We must use wealth wisdom in the choices we make. Start thinking about things that make creating money become second nature. Put your mind to it. Start to think about planting money trees for awesome returns and good fruit. Once we begin to plant seeds of wealth creation the influx of wealth and accumulation will be mind-boggling.

The secret is using what you have "from the neck up". That's where all your untapped value and best resources are. If we keep using that wage/salary part of our body, then we should be rest-assured that you will be earning just that much.

However, if you employ that part of your body that makes limitless amounts of money then you be prepared to make limitless amounts of money. Through purposeful thought one could get an idea that can change the world. There are definitely more great inventors you could very well be one. Everyone of us alive has something we use, do, or think as a result of other people's inventions. Thing is that keeps people spending & as a result become part of that percentage of the population that grows debt and expense trees. Personally I had to learn that money, and not just debt can grow on trees.

Take some time to think. I mean really think! Concentrate on finding seeds for wealth creation and planting them. The more seeds the more trees & the more trees the more potential for fruit!

◆ ◆ ◆

The world is the garden,

your thoughts are the seeds,

you can grow flowers,

or you can grow weeds.

-Unkown

◆ ◆ ◆

EXPENSES VS. ASSETS

If asset & income trees are dried up and brittle but expense & liability trees are in full bloom, then there is trouble in paradise. It is virtually impossible to get ahead. We have given more time and effort to growing debt, instead of growing wealth. Many times at this stage there is barely enough to pay creditors. The minimum balance due on bills are too much. The first thing to do is become aware of any bad decisions. Next is changing those decisions if possible. Once you start thinking different you'll naturally find ways and opportunities to make better decisions. I was surprised how much started and stopped with how I was thinking.

It takes effort to grow either wealth or debt however it takes wisdom and control to place that effort in the right direction. Once you make a conscious decision to change continue the process for more than a few weeks. You will see results. GURANTEED!!!!

ASSETS: CREATE THESE & GROW RICH

Simply put, assets are like orange or banana trees that provide fruit you can eat. Assets put money in your hand. Some may take more time to grow than others.

Even though assets may not grow at the same rate they all eventually mature and yield profit. Picture your assets as seeds that in the right environment germinate and grow. It will be equivalent to planting an almond tree. When the tree begins to bear fruits, you will not be able to finish it. You will be a scrooge if you try to do so.

So also it is with those who have the mentality of developing assets and sowing the seeds for money trees.

Whatever your asset(s) may be, they all started from an idea or thought. The most feasible starting place for any change is your mind.

Your mind is where every seed of thought, which creates everything you see in front of you, comes from.

"Made money" must come from "the neck up". You are the money tree and your thoughts' are the seed or asset. Based on the environment you create your assets will or will not grow.

It's up to you, as with any literal seed; it must be watered, given light, tended to, and sometimes may lose a leaf or two. However, if you do your part you'll have a sturdy tree in the end. The same principles apply in creating wealth.

THE FARMERS' MENTALITY

When a farmer plants seeds in the earth, he does so expecting an abundant return. The farmer expects that by planting seeds, crops will come. He and his family will be able to live off the increase.

Money and ideas are the same way. If you plant them in the earth (figuratively speaking) they will grow.

The farmer realizes that it may not happen overnight. In time, the plants will grow and the fruits will come. It is one of the clichéd laws of nature – where and what you sow, there and that you shall reap.

The farmer, inventor, bank owner, professional athlete, every average person turned billionaire or millionaire simply uses that law to their advantage. They chose a field and started sowing until they reaped.

It does not take money to make money, it takes thought and persistence. The concept of money was nothing more than a thought an idea or seed.

When you grab the idea of money you can plant all the seeds you think of. Ideas are worth more than money. Seeds are ideas, that's why you have to save money in order to buy your idea of pleasure (or whatever you want), which is nothing more than someone else's' idea or seed they planted.

V. Matt Harris

So find your field plant your seeds and start growing your money!

WATCHING YOUR MONEY GROW

Once enough assets have been acquired, your money trees will be in full bloom. At that point, your assets far outweigh your expenditures. When someone asks you if money grows on trees, you will respond in the affirmative. As a result, there is plenty to pay expenses and still live financially free! That's a good result!! Through thought and effort, you can begin to find opportunities for financial independence. Then grow your wealth to be in abundance over all expense.

Everything in life wants you to succeed! There is no lack in nature. Focus on financial independence & freedom. You have the power to get wealth! Exercise it!! Remember money grows on trees! Money is nothing more than an idea that someone came up with. Like a flat-screen, writing pen, car, clothes, light switch, flashlight, towel, synthetic hair and nails you name it. Someone thought of it! It's all worth more than money!

That's why it takes so much money to buy it! So give it some seeds of thought and create an idea that's worth more than money. You are worth more than your paycheck "from the neck up".

◆ ◆ ◆

Happy farming,

V. Matt Harris

@homeboymogul
v.mattharris@gmail.com

www.ingramcontent.com/pod-product-compliance
Lightning Source LLC
Chambersburg PA
CBHW070847220526
45466CB00002B/914